Awaken Your PRESENCE

*7 Keys to Creating More of
What You Really Desire*

BY JEN BUGAJSKY
www.thefreedomkeys.com

Awaken Your Presence
Copyright © 2017 Jennifer Bugajsky

Published by Flower of Life Press, www.floweroflifepress.com

To contact the author: www.TheFreedomKeys.com

All rights reserved. No part of this publication may be reproduced, distributed, or transmitted in any form or by any means, including photocopying, recording, or other electronic or mechanical methods, without the prior written permission of the author, except in the case of brief quotations embodied in critical reviews and certain other noncommercial uses permitted by copyright law.

The content of this book is for general instruction only. Each person's physical, emotional, and spiritual condition is unique. The instruction in this book is not intended to replace or interrupt the reader's relationship with a physician or other mental health professional. Please consult your doctor for matters pertaining to your specific health.

"About Jen" image credit: Bob Briskey, Inspired Beauty Photographer,
www.briskeyphotography.com
All other photos: shutterstock.com

Library of Congress data available upon request.

ISBN-13: 978-0-9863539-4-9

Printed in the United States of America

Introduction

If you are like most women, you will NOT reach your potential, break through the glass ceiling or live the life of your dreams if you are stuck. When you feel stuck, frustrated or overwhelmed, it is a signal you are not in alignment with your true self. When a woman is stuck, she tends to **overthink, over-analyze** and beat herself up, which stops her from taking action and having what she really desires. When you embrace your feminine presence, you tap into a power that allows you to unlock your potential. This personal power enables you to increase your effectiveness and **get the results you want** and that **your team/organization needs,** with more ease and grace instead of pushing to make things happen.

- *Do you feel like you don't get the **support or recognition** you need?*
- *Do you feel some days are an **uphill battle,** pushing hard to get things done?*
- *Do you ever feel like there is **never enough time** to do everything on your list?*
- *Do you feel like a failure because you can't seem to get it all done?*
- *Do you struggle with decisions for fear of making the "wrong" choice?*
- *Do you feel not skilled enough to make the impact you want to make?*
- *Do you go through the motions without purpose or confidence to pursue what is really important to you?*

I have been there, too!

Fear has a way of getting us to over-think or over-analyze and stops us from taking action towards having what we REALLY desire.

I understand…

In this book women are introduced to tools to embody a power that does not intimidate or diminish, but rather attracts and inspires others—a power that emanates from within and does not require using force to achieve one's goals.

If you want to boost your credibility, expand your impact and influence, increase clarity and focus, embrace courageous conversations, effectively deal with conflict, give constructive feedback, set boundaries and stick to them, attain the promotion or new job, create more strategic decisions and/or be seen and tapped for opportunities: personal branding and a strong feminine presence is the key.

Why Does Presence Matter?

If I want to advance my career why does Presence matter?

With the desire to be strong, independent and confident, many women have created a false, inauthentic leadership presence. This lack of authenticity weakens their effectiveness in mobilizing their teams, which reduces engagement and slows business growth. When women are authentically present, they can be present to the needs of others as well as the needs of the organization. They can also reduce stress and create more balance in their lives.

What does it mean to be Feminine in the workplace?

Some people might think that if a woman is assertive or aggressive, she is coming across as "bitchy". Others may look at the complete opposite and think if a woman is not speaking up for herself she is "weak" and not confident enough in her abilities.

With the multitude of roles that women play, many have taken on a more masculine energy. This energy becomes embedded into her everyday activities and can go against the essence of WHO she is. It can stop a woman from creating the influence and impact that she desires.

Women have a natural empowering energy. It is an energy where you don't have to project a certain persona to be noticed or recognized. When a woman embraces her "feminine presence," she shows up grounded, solid and confident. She begins to attract the recognition, opportunities and fulfillment she desires, without forcing or pushing to make things happen.

What is Presence?

Presence is not just about WHAT you SAY or HOW you say it. It's not just about WHAT you DO or HOW you DO IT. It's not struggling or pushing to make things happen. Rather, it's about BEING in the present moment and managing your energy.

Presence is the physical, emotional and energetic way that you show up as WHO YOU ARE. You are "tuned in" and comfortable expressing your true thoughts, feelings, values and potential. When a woman has presence, she shows up confident in who is she is and develops a presence that enables her to be of greater impact and influence.

Presence will allow you to approach stressful situations without anxiety and fear and handle them without regret, doubt or frustration.

"Presence is more than just being there."
–Malcom Forbes

What is Silence?

I have found the secret to what keeps women in overdrive, overwhelm and overthinking, leaving them feeling stressed and unfulfilled and unable to reach their goals. When women are distracted by being BUSY or listening to outside voices, they don't have time to embrace their feminine presence. They unknowingly numb themselves to the truth of WHO they are and sabotage themselves. The key is to tap into their feminine presence and learn to embrace SILENCE.

According to Webster, the definition of SILENCE is being quiet and still. I refer to SILENCE as a tool to tap into your inner wisdom. It is allowing yourself to be grounded and centered and use all of your senses to make strategic intuitive decisions that allow you to attract more of what you want and less of what you don't want—so that you get the results you desire for yourself and your organization.

Women have everything that they need inside. They don't need another degree or certification. They don't have to prove anything to anyone. But how do women tap into that wisdom? It begins with SILENCE.

So, how do you embrace silence?

In this program, you will dive deeper into each of the 7 powerful steps to unlock and awaken your feminine presence, power and potential.

You will begin making small changes that will help you to STOP overthinking and listening to the voices telling yourself you are NOT strong enough, deserving enough or confident enough.

You will START to make more powerful decisions by 1) learning to live in the present moment and to be observant rather than judging, 2) taking bold, courageous actions and 3) building your confidence muscle so you can step into your authentic self and play a bigger game in life and business.

The next page outlines 7 key affirmations you can to start your day with each morning. You will also have worksheets for each chapter at the back of the book to assist in building your "presence" muscle. Using this book along with the tools provided will help you to unlock YOUR presence to get the results YOU desire and what your team/organization needs.

"Everything that's created comes out of silence. Your thoughts emerge from the nothingness of silence. Your words come out of this void. Your very essence emerged from emptiness. All creativity requires some stillness."
–Dr. Wayne Dyer

Silence

*Your body is wise and holds keys
to your transformation. Begin
accessing this wisdom with these gentle,
powerful affirmations.
Trust her wisdom.
It all begins with Silence.*

STOP AND NOTICE — *I AM still. I take time to pause and notice. I am receptive to the messages that are available to me.*

INTENTION — *I AM open and curious. I set intentions and pray for my own needs.*

LISTEN — *I AM awake and present. I allow myself to notice with no judgment, just pure awareness through all of my senses.*

EMOTIONS — *I AM vulnerable. I allow myself to feel. I process through my feelings and emotions.*

NEW BEGINNINGS — *I AM brave. I embrace the lessons and allow myself to follow my heart.*

CHOICE — *I AM forgiving. I choose to let go and release the strongholds I have placed on myself and others.*

EXPRESS YOUR SOUL — *I AM love. I believe in myself. I love and respect myself by practicing daily self care rituals.*

AN INTRODUCTION TO PRESENCE
S – Stop and Notice

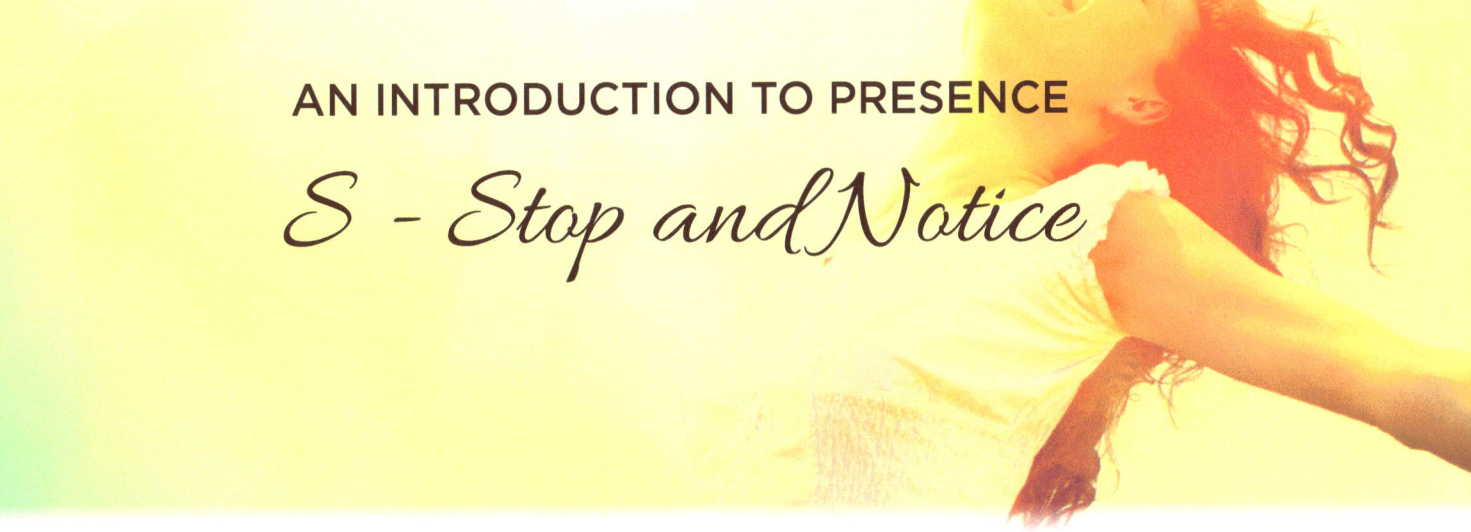

- *Do you ever feel like there is more to do in the day than the hours available?*
- *Do you find yourself going from back to back meetings or activities with little time to eat or go to the bathroom?*
- *Do you ever find yourself scattered and rushing to get things done?*
- *Do you wonder where the time went and how you are going to do everything on your list?*

The first step is learning how to **STOP and NOTICE. Build in more times of pause and be mindful to "tune into" what is going on in the present.**

In our busy lives it can be hard to see what is going on around us if we are constantly on the go. We don't take enough time to stop and smell the roses. Busy women tend to be in control of the household, work a part-time or full time job, be involved in volunteer activities and take care of friends, family and loved ones. This leaves them little to no time left to care for themselves.

The hard truth is that when a woman puts her needs aside, she doesn't have the energy to meet the demands of the day. Her productivity suffers and she becomes ineffective. She thinks she is working really hard to meet everyone else's demands and strives to please others, but ends up depleting herself.

When a woman strives to "DO IT ALL", she ends up finding herself feeling **exhausted and overwhelmed.** She lacks the energy to make the difference she wants to make in her family, workplace or community. She is not running in her highest vibration and ends up feeling, stuck, disengaged and unfulfilled. She limits herself and her potential. **She needs to identify the warning signs of when her mind and body are on overdrive.**

When women are authentically present to their own feminine nature, they can be present to their own needs as well as the needs of those around them including the needs of their family, community or organization.

AN INTRODUCTION TO PRESENCE
S - Stop and Notice

The first step to increasing your energy levels and reducing stress is to be **OPEN** to the possibilities of doing things differently. Creating an opening to become more engaged and fulfilled in life by learning to STOP and NOTICE. It is not about working hard and pleasing others, it is about building in times of pause into our lives. **We need to work smart and hard by learning how to do MORE with less.**

It is OK to not be busy all of the time. In fact rest and play are a necessity and not a luxury. When we are resting, our body and mind are still. When we are at play, our mind and body are enjoying. In both instances we are in the moment. We are not worried about the past, or concerned about the future, we are literally experiencing the moment as it is. **We begin to understand that taking time for ourselves is NOT selfish, it is necessary and healthy, not just for ourselves, but for our family and our community.**

It is in these moments that we not only enjoy, but come up with some of the most creative ideas that benefit not just ourselves but others with whom we connect. When we embrace the concept of being present, we are able to tap into an energy and power that is greater than we could ever possibly imagine.

THE POWER OF INTENTION TO ACHIEVE GOALS
I - Intention

I sat really hard when writing this section, as I felt it was really important to highlight some areas that might be controversial, in both a corporate and church setting. I chose to include them because I believe it's important to be real. My goal is not to please anyone by the language I use or don't use, but rather my mission in life is speak my own truth and empower other women in finding their own voice.

So I thought long and hard about the word intention and reflected back to childhood. I don't know about you, but growing up we set goals and intentions at certain points during the year typically around new years' and different points during the academic school year, however, I was taught to pray daily and focus on the needs of others. We recited beautiful prayers of worship and thanksgiving for all of the amazing things God has provided in our in life. We also prayed for the needs of others especially those who were sick, poor, dying or really in need of help.

I found it interesting that we prayed daily for others and set intentions a few times a year. **What does it really mean to have an intention?**

- ***Intention***-a determination or clear formulation to deliberately act in a certain way
- ***Goal***-the object of a person's ambition or effort, an aim or desired result
- ***Dream***-a series of thoughts, images and sensations occurring in a person's mind
- ***Desire***-a strong feeling of wanting or wishing for something to happen
- ***Prayer***-a solemn request for help; an expression of thanks addressed to God or an object of worship
- ***Prayer intention***-spoken or unspoken petitions to God or the greater Universe, an invocation to or act seeking spiritual connection by asking for something we want (for ourselves or others)

What I have found is that people regularly **set intentions for themselves (annually or quarterly),** but don't always focus on the follow up required to achieve their goals. However, they **pray for others on a regular daily basis.** It got me to really seriously think about the meaning and intention of prayer.

I believe that God answers all of our prayers, but sometimes we are just not

THE POWER OF INTENTION TO ACHIEVE GOALS
I - Intention

AWAKE to listen for the answers that could be right in front of us. In my experience, many women don't realize that we can ask for intentions for ourselves; for our own dreams and desires that he placed in our hearts. Prayer is not just for the needy, sick or poor. There is absolutely amazing power in praying for others, however, I want to encourage you to take the time and PRAY FOR YOURSELF too. I don't mean this in a selfish way, but rather as a way of saying, I need and am asking for help in this area of my life.

It is NOT selfish to pray and ask for your own needs and desires. It is similar to setting a focused intention asking for what you desire.

Just imagine how different our lives could be if we shifted our thinking on how we pray and set intentions:

When you pray, here are a few things to think about:
- *Do you spend time daily in prayer?*
- *Who or what do you pray for?*
- *Do you recite prayers or do you customize your prayer?*
- *Do you find more of your prayers are for others than yourself?*
- *Do you ask God or a higher power to show you what he wants for you?*
- *Are your prayers focused on your desires and will for someone else's life or on their hopes and dreams for their life?*
- *Do you ask to bring out your talents strengths and gifts so that you can use them use to make a bigger impact in the world?*
- *Do you ask for your children to be shown their gifts and talents so that you can help nurture the desires within their own hearts?*

Some of us fear that we should not be asking for wants and we should only focus on needs. Other times we pray for things we WANT, with the intention that we are longing for something so much, that we literally end up setting the intention to create the *opposite* of what we really desire. We LONG so much that we create "lack of" in our life. Others have so many worries about the future that they end up praying for the worry. Again setting intentions and praying for things that

THE POWER OF INTENTION TO ACHIEVE GOALS

I - Intention

they don't want. It's important for us to **learn how to choose our language carefully and understand how "wanting" and "worrying"** can create the exact opposite effect of what our heart truly desires.

I have also learned that sometimes we can be too attached to the outcome of our desires, that we limit the possibilities of what COULD BE. When you have a prayer, intention or desire, first you have to have a dream and set the intention, then you need to visualize the outcome without being attached the HOW, then sit back and allow yourself to be open to receive the answer to your prayers or intentions. It is with focused intention that our lives bloom.

Think about a flower. It needs focused attention daily. If you didn't water it and give it sunlight daily, it wouldn't grow, it would slowly die. It is the same for our souls. We need focused attention daily to our intentions, and then when our souls are fed, they will blossom into the unlimited potential that we desire. Focused attention can be through intentions or prayers, but the key is to create the focus on a regular basis.

Each one of us has a different foundation in what we believe when it comes to faith, prayer and a higher power. Some people call it God, The Universe, Spirit, The Light, A Higher Power, whatever it is for you, I believe and have seen that when we tune into the source of Truth, amazing things begin to happen in our lives. The Freedom Keys is not about any one particular religion or faith however, I will share examples from my own personal experience and faith journey as examples that were keys to my personal transformation.

Religion is an out-word expression of a set of strong beliefs and traditional practices. Each religion has a variety of different beautiful rituals that help you to worship and celebrate with yourself and with your community. I am not promoting or knocking any religion, as they all have a beautiful place in the world.

Spirituality is learning to focus inward and not looking for advice and seeking approval from others, but rather the source of Truth. I believe that we have everything that we need already within ourselves. We just have to ask for what we need and listen for the answer. So how do we do that?

First, believe in a higher power, and trust in your faith. Learn how to be still, relax and tune into your heart space. Your heart knows the answer. It is only in this

THE POWER OF INTENTION TO ACHIEVE GOALS

I - Intention

place of silence that we are able to listen to source. If our head and other people's beliefs or opinions get in the way, we can be stuck and confused. We were all born with intuition, but many of us have lost our way of getting in tune with our "gut instincts". We can all learn to re-embrace that inner wisdom.

How do you tune into your heart?

Think of a time when you listened to your gut. How did you feel? What are some ways that you can experience SILENCE?

- *Meditation (There are many forms of meditation)*
- *Reading the Word (God speaks to us through his word)*
- *Going to a Church Service (Worshiping as a community)*
- *Walking in nature and observe*
- *Be Still and Listen – Discern what comes from God vs. ego*

God reaches us through many forms, but the key is to be SILENT and listen. Praying is talking to God, but just as with any relationship it's a two way street, and we MUST learn how to make the time in our days to listen.

USING PRESENCE TO FUEL PRODUCTIVITY
L - Listen

Have you ever driven somewhere and out of habit, went the way you always go and realized you had to turn around because you missed your turn. Or better yet, have you ever been on a call where you were going through the next steps of a project, you ask for an answer and dead silence. You think to yourself, is anyone listening to me? And the person on the other end says I'm sorry, can you please repeat that?

- *Are you paying attention? Are you really listening?*
- *Are you thinking and doing and not allowing yourself time to step back and observe?*
- *Are you too busy to notice and miss the answer right in front of you?*
- *Are you making good decisions or just checking things off the list?*

If you are not fully present and engaged in the moment you can say yes to something when you should have said no. When we are seeking first to understand, we are paying attention. We are **AWAKE** in the present moment. We are not doing something else or thinking about our next response, we are fully engaged. **Learn how you can boost your credibility and reputation by being in the present moment.**

When you are multi-tasking it is difficult to be fully engaged in just one thing. However, in our fast pace busy world, women tend to multi-task to squeeze as much as possible. There is a sense of satisfaction when you can cross things off the "to do" list. You feel accomplished and productive. However, just because you do something doesn't mean that you were fully engaged and that the best decisions were made.

Replace multi-tasking with tuning into your senses. If you think about tuning into a radio station, if you are not tuned into the right station number, you will hear static. That is the same with our lives. In order to really hear the connection, we need to "tune in" and learn how to pay attention and **AWAKEN to the signs that are all around us.** To create a shift we need to DO SOMETHING different. So what does that look like?

When you become grounded and are in tune with your inner wisdom, you are open to new possibilities. All five senses are amazing tools that enable us to listen to that inner wisdom.

How many of you pay close attention to all of your senses? You already have everything you need to know inside of you. The best way to tap into that awareness is to become in tune with and explore your senses. Your body is a guide to getting in

USING PRESENCE TO FUEL PRODUCTIVITY
L - Listen

touch with your inner wisdom. You might be thinking, how is paying attention to my senses going to help me get all of the things done on my "to do" list?! How is this going to help me in my job?

I challenge you, to be OPEN to the possibility that when you begin to work the muscle of awareness, you will begin to notice things around you in countless ways. **You will learn how to see the clues and the breadcrumbs that are leaving a trail for you.** Begin with some simple things you can do to practice being more mindful every day.

How do you tap into the senses in our body? These are just a few examples, but there are many more we can dive into. First, you need to be still, quiet and focus. Then you can "tune into" your senses.

SEE: First imagine your dreams, before they can become a reality.

- *WORK: Create a vision for your personal or team objectives. Rather than just putting the vision in words, have you thought about creating a business vision board for yourself or your team?*
- *HOME: How often do you wonder or imagine? As kids we were taught to play and use our imagination to create, how often do we do this as adults at home? If you could create anything for your life right now, what would it be? Use nature as a way to remind you of appreciation to beauty of creation.*

FEEL: Stop feeling numb and allow yourself to feel and be in touch with your physical body. All disease first begins in our energetic field before it manifests in the body, so when it gets to the physical, PAY ATTENTION. This isn't something that occurred overnight, it's been building for a long time.

- *WORK: Close your eyes and breathe. Feel the energy around you. Get present to it. Put your hands over your heart, or even over your face as you feel the energy come back into your body.*
- *HOME: Get a massage. Allow yourself the time and space to relax and distress.*

Overall, feel what your body is telling you. Do you feel blessed, grateful and hopeful? Or do you feel tired, overwhelmed, hungry, or cranky? Are you getting enough sleep, exercise or nutrition? These are things that you can identify both at work and at home that have an impact on each other. If you are feeling anxiety at home, you bring that into the workplace. If you are feeling frustrated at work, you bring that home to your family environment. Pay attention and track the following habits:

- Water / Nutrition and Food
- Sleep
- Exercise
- Meditation
- Triggers and emotional responses

USING PRESENCE TO FUEL PRODUCTIVITY
L - Listen

SMELL/BREATHE: Take the time to smell the roses.

- *WORK: Stop and breathe. Before you send that email, before you call that customer, take a moment to breathe so that you can be mindful in the words you choose and in your next step. Breathe out the negative energy and breathe in clean energy that will enable you to think more clearly.*
- *HOME: Do you stop and smell the scents/odors inside and outside your home? Do you know how powerful our olfactory system is to our environment? It is the home of emotions, motivation, hormones, regulation of memories, "fight or flight" responses and sexual arousal.*
- *Remove toxins from the air you breathe and replace with clean air or aromatic oils. Toxins in the air negatively impact our mood and physical well-being, just as clean aromatic air can have a positive impact on mood, cognitive, psychological or physical wellbeing.*

TASTE: When was the last time you truly enjoyed your food?

- *WORK: Sit down and eat a meal. Don't eat breakfast, lunch and dinner while working. Your body and mind need a break. Pick one meal where you will make a shift and take a break from working while eating.*
- *HOME: Take the time to really enjoy rather than scarf down your food. You may find that you might not eat as much, or that if you savor that piece of chocolate, you only need one bite and not a whole box.*

HEAR: Listen to the sounds all around you. Hear what you "THINK" and "SAY" to yourself

- *WORK: Pay attention to what people say and how they say it. Observe and hear the messages that might be hidden in a conversation. (It might be words, sounds or silence)*
- *HOME: Hear what you think and say to yourself. Do you say things like "I can't do it, I am not good enough or this stinks" Even though you don't say something, if you think it, you are still bringing it into reality.*
- *Be impeccable with your word.*

When you are able to awaken to the messages that are ALL AROUND, you are able to hear your inner voice and **craft more informed and strategic decisions for your business and your life.**

RECOGNIZING AND OVERCOMING BLOCKS TO PRESENCE
PART 1
E - Emotions

Feelings are real and to be an effective leader it is important to understand the messages that our feelings are telling us. Our feelings are triggers that help us determine if we are in alignment with our goals, objectives, dreams and desires. Feelings are not right or wrong. They are here to teach us lessons. But many times we can allow our emotions to get the best of us by projecting or by burying what we feel.

- *Have you ever worn your emotions on your sleeve? Or do you bury them?*
- *Have you ever criticized or judged yourself or others for how they feel?*
- *Are you afraid to express your thoughts and opinions in fear of what others will think?*
-

Let's understand the REAL issue. When you are grounded and tuned into your inner wisdom, the TRUTH is revealed. Once you connect your higher guidance and become aware that your **feelings are meant to guide you on your path,** there is no longer a need to be afraid of them. **The key is to acknowledge and embrace these emotions, don't deny or resist them.** For what you resist will persist. Many people bury their feelings, however, when you resist what those feelings are meant to reveal to you, they will continue to show up in different ways, until you learn the lesson that was meant for you. **Embrace the lesson under the trigger. Your feelings and emotions are not right or wrong, they just are. Accept them with no judgment.**

When you open yourself up to the truth, sometimes you learn things that you didn't want to know, or bring up old wounds that you really wanted to forget. At this point, the natural tendency is to ignore or deny those feelings. Saying things like, that is in the past and it doesn't really matter. It is much easier to go back to the way things were because you are comfortable in what you know and are afraid to face your fears.

The challenge with this pattern is that you are unconsciously allowing the fears and the limiting beliefs that were programmed into your beings to rule your life. You end up creating stories around

RECOGNIZING AND OVERCOMING BLOCKS TO PRESENCE
PART 1

E - Emotions

events that have occurred to protect yourself from your fears. And these feelings will continue to show up and trigger you in numerous ways until you come to a point where you allow yourself to feel the emotion and learn the lesson to **recognize what is out of alignment between your reality and your goals and intentions.** You can learn how to identify patterns in your triggers.

The great news is that God does not want fear for you. He wants love, abundance, harmony and freedom for all. The subconscious mind and soul knows everything about your life purpose, however your ego wants to be in control and not allow you to go there. So when you get triggered by something that happens in your life, and your emotions start to fly, remember it is OK to allow yourself to feel, **accept positive and negative feelings for what they are.** Don't try to bury your emotions. There is healing in sharing and expressing your feelings.

If it were easy to tap into our feelings, everyone would be doing it, all the time. The good news is that it is possible and we are seeing more and more people tapping into their source energy to identify triggers and blocks that are holding them back from achieving their dreams and goals. This STEP here is sometimes where people give up. You question what it is that you are sensing and feeling. Your mind tries to take over and you tell yourself that you should or shouldn't feel a certain way. You judge yourself for what are perceived as "negative" feelings. How many times have you heard a parent say to a child, don't cry, there is no reason to feel that way? Many people have been conditioned to bury their feelings inside, but the opposite is what you need. ALLOW yourself to feel.

I have used a variety of different strategies in allowing myself to feel and NOT deny the truth and begin to tap into the wisdom underneath the surface.

- *Breathing and putting my hand on my heart*
- *Journaling*
- *Meditation (Guided and Unguided)*
- *Feminine Presence Meditation TM*

RECOGNIZING AND OVERCOMING BLOCKS TO PRESENCE PART 1

E - Emotions

- *EFT–Emotional Freedom Technique ™*
- *Energy Healing Massage/Intuitive or Energy Coaching*

It is important to note the difference between **feeling** our emotions and **acting on** our emotions. Emotions are not right or wrong, they just are. Feeling the emotion of anger is one thing, with no judgment, but the acting out of an emotion is different. If we allow ourselves to feel the emotions and have the courage to work through them, we will find it is easier to move on. Our emotions will no longer be holding us back.

It is usually the things that trigger us the most, and bring up deep feelings that can be our greatest teachers. Look at your triggers and feelings as a gift. Embrace them all! They are meant to teach you a lesson. When you ignore them, they will continue to come back and haunt you, as if they never went away and they will show up in a different place in a different way, until you learn the lesson.

It is only when you begin to embrace the trigger and the feelings that you begin to uncover the lesson underneath it all.

You will find that many of the challenges in the workplace can be tied back to some type of feeling or emotion that has not been expressed or properly dealt with. If employees learn how to manage their emotions and learn the lessons from them, they will be more productive and have improved relationships in the workplace and at home.

RECOGNIZING AND OVERCOMING BLOCKS TO PRESENCE
PART 2
N – New Beginnings

Our brain is like a computer system, information needs to be programmed into the system and the application with then function based on what was input into the program. If there is a desire to enhance or change the functionality of the system, someone has to physically go into the computer program and code the changes. It doesn't happen automatically. If I think about the project development life cycle, there are many phases:

1. Identify the project and need for enhancement
2. Review and analyze the requirements
3. Visualize and create the design
4. Open up the code and reprogram the system
5. Test out the Changes and tweak as necessary
6. Implement the new functionality into the system

The same is true for our lives. Many of us don't' realize that we only use 5 – 10% of our consciousness; the other 90- 95% is subconscious, we run on autopilot. Our lives are run based on our subconscious and what was programmed into our mind years ago. If nothing new is programmed into the mind, it will continue to function based on the information that has been stored in the mind.

The biggest reason we don't do things is because we are afraid. We are afraid of failure, letting someone down, not being good enough, not being perfect etc… These fears block us from stepping up to our full potential. **How do we identify the lies that are getting in our way and overcome these emotional blocks?**

1. Identify what events are triggering your fear and getting in the way?
2. Ask the question, how is the fear serving me? What do I need to learn from it?
3. Stop resisting; Step up and embrace the fear; acknowledge its existence
4. Be courageous to feel the fear, embrace your vulnerability and do it anyway

Becoming aware and tapping into the depths of our truth, allow us to acknowledge and begin to accept the lies

RECOGNIZING AND OVERCOMING BLOCKS TO PRESENCE
PART 2
N - New Beginnings

we have been holding that have been running the show. There could be things that happened to us as a child, teenager, and/or adult where we created vows and intentions to protect ourselves from fear. **What we begin to start realizing is that these stories and fears in our head can be reprogrammed.**

Our bodies are wise and help us to determine our own truth. We have everything we need inside of us and if we tap into our inner wisdom, our body can share with us things we never realized that were blocking our ability to face our fears.

In the book Rapid Change, I talk about how my body just told me things that I needed to know. When I wasn't sure if I should listen to my body, I went back to the toolkit I was taught as a child. For example, I went to the chapel to pray. I knew God would NOT lie to me in the chapel. I didn't think he would lie to me while praying in my house either, but I thought if I was in God's house, he surely wouldn't lie to me.

The key was remaining open to what was being revealed to me. There was another time, when I was afraid of what my body was telling me and I went to confession to let go and release the heavy burden. It was a powerful experience that allowed me to receive messages I needed to hear. Whatever your faith foundation, use the tools that you were taught to help you get into deeper communion with your soul. Tapping into our emotions is an amazing tool to clear out the clutter in our head space and allow ourselves to be free to stay open and listen to our hearts.

When we are able to recognize the fears that are holding us back, we can take action. We can **stop avoiding conflict** and do the things we fear most. **Embrace your vulnerability**. I know that is easier said than down, however, the important thing to remember is that IT IS A PROCESS and there is no finish line. It gets easier to overcome obstacles overtime, but when you are first learning how to clear blocks and limiting beliefs it can be scary. **Seeking support and recognizing when you need help is a strength. Embrace courageous conversations and step into the authentic leader you are.** When you first begin to notice a trigger, have the courage to pause and reflect on your own. Use some of the tools men-

RECOGNIZING AND OVERCOMING BLOCKS TO PRESENCE
PART 2

N - New Beginnings

tioned in "L" for listen and see if you can pay attention to your own inner wisdom and uncover the lesson for you. If after looking at this yourself, you are unable to identify the pattern and the lesson seek out a coach who can help guide you through the process. The biggest lesson I have learned is not to be afraid of what I might learn. Stop resisting and avoiding conflict, as it will just keep repeating itself. **Feel the fear and do it anyway.**

In my own personal experience, my body showed me through various ways, answers that guided me on my path. We will sometimes be tested to see how bad we want something and how far we will go. I read a story the morning I wrote this from the book Jesus Calling. It was a story about a man who went to see Jesus, but they couldn't get in. His friends were ready to leave and they were about to give up, but the man said NO. There has to be a way. So they lowered him down with a rope to see Jesus. This was an act of faith. When you set an intention, Source wants to know that you are ready to act and have full and complete trust and faith, especially when it might seem hopeless.

Allow yourself to break free of the chains that have been holding you back from your true potential. When you tap into the depths of your soul, you will begin to see yourself transform right in front of your eyes. When you learn how to express your feelings you can create a new situation or outcome instead of resisting, reacting and creating more drama.

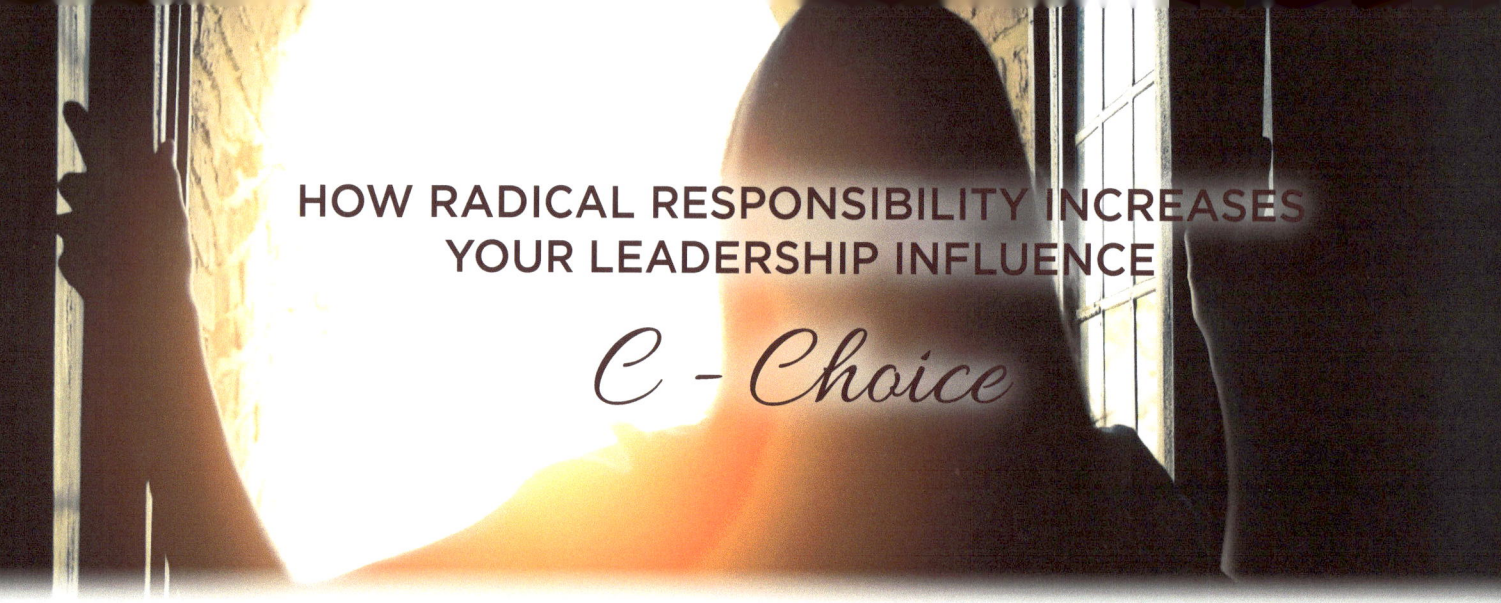

HOW RADICAL RESPONSIBILITY INCREASES YOUR LEADERSHIP INFLUENCE

C – Choice

It is so much easier to point the finger at others when things aren't going well, but before you do, take a look at what lesson might be there for you. **Embrace compassion and stop blaming others for your performance of lack of performance.** When there are issues on the team and you see a conflict with another team member, I challenge you to think about why it bothers you. Why does it trigger you? What lesson is there to learn for you from this person's actions?

In the laws of gravity, what comes around goes around. So if you are witnessing a behavior in someone else that makes your blood boil, take some time to seriously think about what that really means to you. Yes, it may be a fact that they are behaving a certain way and it's not your job to fix them, however, the feelings that you feel by observing their behavior are telling you something about you. YES. I am going to say that again. When you observe someone else's perceived negative behaviors, **take a look in the mirror and see what lesson there is for YOU.** I know this is a tough pill to swallow, however I encourage you to wake up and **accept radical responsibility.**

Once you become aware of your responsibility in a challenging situation or have identified things that might be holding you back, it is time to release and let go. There is no reason to continue carrying the burden on your own. You may believe that you have a good reason to protect yourself from the past, but we need to let go of the old and create space for the new. If we try to stay in control, resist adversity and do it all on our own, it is very likely that you continue to see the same lesson repeated in your life. You are going to make life a struggle and in turn more difficulties arise for yourself.

Don't get me wrong, I don't mean that you will never see failures or setbacks. Rather what I mean is when you stop resisting and let go, you are no longer allowing false stories to hold you back. **Pause the guilt button and stop judging yourself.** Release painful things from the past, limiting beliefs, excuses you have

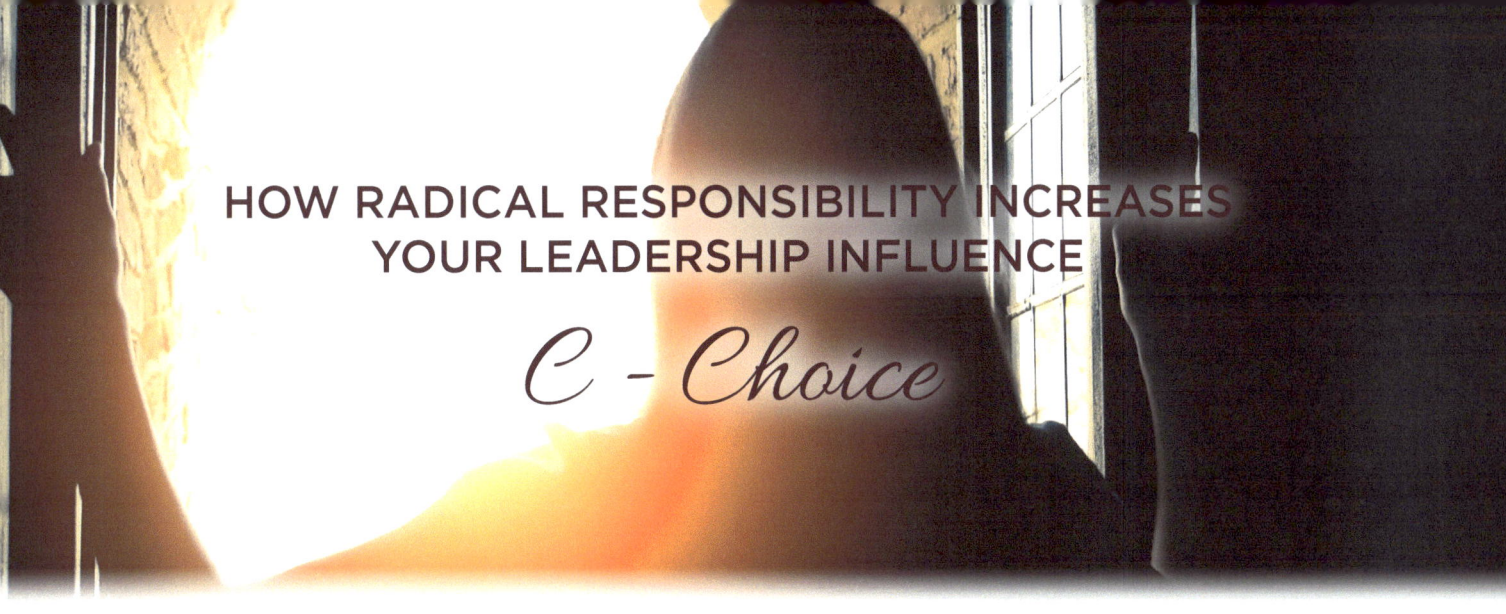

HOW RADICAL RESPONSIBILITY INCREASES YOUR LEADERSHIP INFLUENCE

C - Choice

used that stop you from moving forward. **When you identify what is no longer serving you and embrace the lesson, you create space for new ideas to emerge.**

We need to learn how to 'Forgive and Let Go". I actually had a vision of my deceased grandfather about 4 years ago with a message. He wanted me to share the message of Forgive and Let Go. It was such a profound and powerful message. It was the very first time I meditated and I didn't even realize I was doing it, but the very next day, I could see and feel his presence guiding my path.

In the Catholic Church, "The Our Father" talks about forgiveness "Forgive us our trespasses, as we forgive those who trespass against us". It doesn't just talk about forgiving others, the first phrase talks about forgiving ourselves. We need to learn how to forgive ourselves. It's one thing to go to confession and say you are sorry for something, but there is a complete difference, in digging deep and really knowing the profound reasons behind what is holding you back. The first step is radical self-acceptance and responsibility. You first must take ownership for your own stuff.

In the book *Rapid Change*, I shared that I had prayed for my marriage many times. I had gone to confession before and asked for forgiveness, with no luck. I was also part of a marriage encounter group where we prayed all the time for our marriage, but it just wasn't happening. There was something UNDERNEATH the layers of what I was saying I was sorry for, but I didn't know it. We need to learn the real benefit of releasing, letting go and accepting and loving ourselves. It is then and only then that we are ready for the next step. Many of us hold on so tightly and think we are letting go, when in actuality we are not. **When you BELIEVE, and I mean truly believe with the eyes of compassion, you are able to let go.** When you show compassion to yourself, you open the door to self-forgiveness. We all make mistakes and have fears and anxieties. Self-compassion teaches us to be gentle and forgiving of our own thoughts and feelings, so that we can truly embrace the deepest versions of our self.

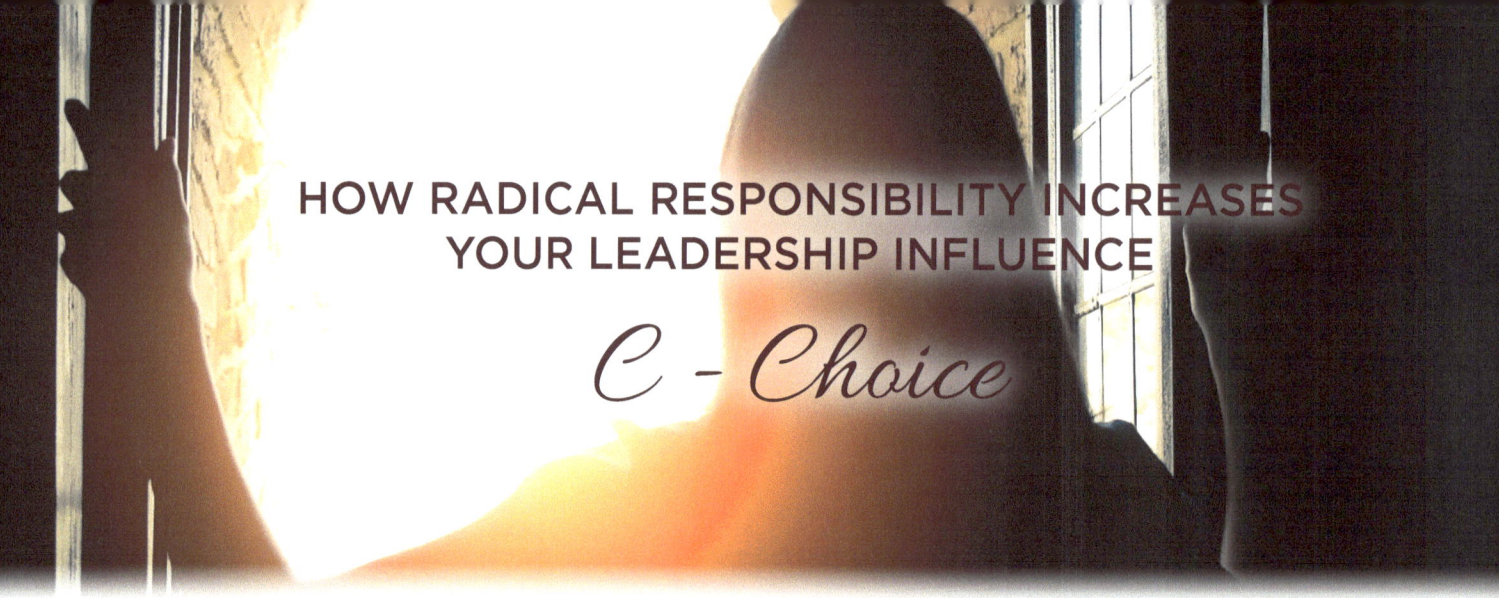

HOW RADICAL RESPONSIBILITY INCREASES YOUR LEADERSHIP INFLUENCE

C - Choice

When you are able to take full responsibility and ownership for what might be holding you back, you can eliminate any self-sabotaging behaviors. You will begin to have more compassion for yourself and others, and you will **boost your credibility** and begin to create a true sense of appreciation and collaboration in the organization.

If I have a team member who I am frustrated with because they are not following through on commitments, they don't seem to take responsibility for their project and appear to be disrespectful at times, **STOP and become aware of what they are trying to reveal to you.** Your energy vibration attracted this type of energy, so even though they may have development issues, the fact that you get triggered by their behaviors means there is wisdom there for you to dive deeper.

BUILDING, MAINTAINING AND EMBODYING CONFIDENCE

E - Express

The world needs more women to step up their game and find their voice. **When you begin to eliminate self-sabotaging behaviors, you harness your untapped potential and move into a new phase of authentic leadership. You gain credibility, respect and results.** This phase is all about increasing your confidence, showcasing your abilities, and believing in yourself.

Once you have let go of whatever has been holding you back, you can celebrate and rejoice. Give yourself permission to live your passion with integrity, appreciate your talents and achieve authentic success. Self-expression is your birthright. Each and every one of you, are all unique individuals with talents and gifts to bring to the world. The only way to tap into that creativity is to express your true authentic voice.

Women can be so hard on themselves and don't praise themselves often enough. Even as you start to eliminate limiting beliefs, there can be phases of self-doubt that creep in saying things, like, "Can I really do this". Do I really have it in me? What if I fail?

If you truly have a desire to live out your goals, dreams and intentions, for your life and the company that you serve, you must have faith and believe. WHAT IF IT'S POSSIBLE... **When you eliminate self-doubting behaviors and believe in yourself with conviction,** you are seen, you are heard and you attract the energy that you desire that enables you to achieve success and live out your dreams.

How many of you take time every day to celebrate and recognize yourself? It is a concept where many of us struggle. We need to have more compassion for ourselves and express our truth.

We all know how it feels to be recognized and rewarded. It feels great! We love when others give us a complement and say nice things about us. However, it is just as important to do the same thing for ourselves. Do you find it easier to pay someone else a complement? When you look at yourself, do you begin to criticize and judge? **Learn how to embrace celebrating your own successes without being boastful.** It all begins with you beginning to appreciate the value that you provide and bring to the table. Once you

BUILDING, MAINTAINING AND EMBODYING CONFIDENCE

E - Express

believe in yourself and see the gifts, talents and unique value, you provide, others will begin to notice.

Think about the following:
- When someone gives you a complement, do you graciously say thank you, or do you say something like, it is no big deal.
- Do you punish yourself instead of reward yourself?
- What are some things you do to celebrate yourself?
- How do you show yourself love every day?
- Do you honor, appreciate, love and respect yourself?
- What are the characteristics and qualities you use to describe yourself?

The last piece of expressing your voice is learning to embrace and believe in your own value and worth. It is so easy to compare ourselves to others. Society has molded us to want to know where we stand in conjunction with others. We want to be seen as valuable, as good enough. We want to receive a high rating and be viewed as an exceptional performer, wife, mother, friend etc...

When you speak your truth and live your passion, you celebrate, honor, cherish and respect yourself for who you are. You begin a radical transformation and achieve authentic success. You must value your own self-worth. No one can do that for you. **Stop comparing yourself to others and embrace the power of acceptance.** If you are your own authentic self, there is NO competition. There is nothing about being superior to another person. True nobility is being superior to the person you once were.

*"I am in competition with no one. I run my own race. I have no desire to play the game of being better than anyone, in any way, shape or form. I just aim to improve, to be better than I was before.
That's me and I am FREE."*
– Jenny G. Perry

Girls compete with each other. Women empower one another. My entire journey has been about learning how to honor, appreciate, love and respect myself. But it all began with SILENCE.

"When you know yourself you are empowered, but when you accept yourself, you are invincible."
– Tina Lifford

Workbook

S = STOP AND NOTICE
I
L
E
N
C
E

Module 1

Stop & Notice: Self Discovery Awareness

Use this practice exercise to let your mind rest. Practice allowing yourself to be in the present moment at any point in the day. Your homework is to STOP and NOTICE.

1. Pick a time during the day where you would like to create more awareness. (i.e. morning, during workday, evening, or one the weekend).
2. Pick one suggestion for how you can pause and begin to notice. Don't be afraid of long pauses or periods of silence. There is great wisdom to be learned in our own stillness.
3. STOP and NOTICE

Practice Exercise: STOP, create SILENCE and become more aware...

The goal is: to be open to ALLOW yourself to be in the present at any given moment.
The goal is NOT: to worry or feel guilty about the past or the future.

How do you know when to create time to be more mindful?

There is no scientific formula for when each person should silence their minds. Here are a few suggestions to get you started:

- Begin your day with "SILENCE"
- Schedule "SILENCE breaks" in your calendar (begin w 5-10 min)
- When you feel stressed
- When you notice that you haven't had a break during the day
- When you feel frustrated, angry or upset about something at home or work
- When you are ready to begin the transition between work and home
- End your day with "SILENCE"

How can you create more mindfulness in the busyness of your workday?

- Take a break
- Close eyes and take a few deep breaths
- Place hand over heart and breathe
- Walk in nature/ Go for a walk;
- Listen to a favorite song
- Change the scenery: walk away from your desk and go sit in a place that is cozy, warm and inviting and just soak up the energy
- Make yourself a cup of tea or a light healthy snack
- Write down things you are grateful for
- Dance - Allow your body to move and flow with the beat of the music
- Stretch - Move your neck
- Decompress and take warm heat and wrap around your neck; close your eyes and relax your face, neck, upper chest and back muscles
- Try aromatherapy and keep essential oils flowing

Stop & Notice:
Self Discovery Awareness

Module 1

S = STOP AND NOTICE
I
L
E
N
C
E

What are some other activities you can do to enhance your awareness and deepen your experience of self-discovery?

- Meditation
- Exercise/Aerobic Activity
- Journaling
- Visualization
- Call a friend (Sometimes you may need social connection)
- Going to church to pray
- Taking a bubble bath
- Read a book (If it takes your mind away from thinking)
- Do something you absolutely love
- Play
- Laugh
- Take a nap
- Get a massage

S = STOP AND NOTICE
I = INTENTION
L
E
N
C
E

Module 2

Intention Analysis

Who and what do you set intentions for? Typically individuals set intentions for the year, but how often do you revisit your intentions on a regular basis? When I think about intentions, I don't just think about goals for the year, but I also relate that to prayer intentions which I think about on a daily basis.

Prayer intentions are spoken or unspoken petitions to God or the greater Universe. It is an invocation or act seeking spiritual connection by asking for something we want. (Whether for ourselves or others)

Begin thinking about the things that you pray and ask for on a regular basis. Many people focus on praying for the needs of others or for those who are ill or in need. But how much time do you focus on praying and asking for yourself and your own needs and desires. Take some time to jot down off of the top of your head any intentions that come to mind on things that you pray and ask for on a regular basis.

FAMILY	OTHERS	SELF

Intention Analysis

Module 2

S = STOP AND NOTICE
I = INTENTION
L
E
N
C
E

Do you ever pray, worry and get caught up in what might happen? Worry is the opposite of faith. It is like praying or setting an intention for what you don't want. It steals your peace, physically wears you out and can even make you sick.

Reflection: I encourage you to reflect on what you have noticed about the intentions you set on a regular basis.

- What comes to mind when you think about asking for your own needs and desires?
- Are you so focused on praying for the needs of others that you forget to pray and ask for support and help for your own needs?
- Do you feel guilty about setting intentions and asking for your own needs?
- Is your list for others long and the one for yourself short?

Remember there is no judgment. There is no right or wrong answer. Just stop and notice what you observe. Sometimes we have a hard time asking for what we want, because we don't know what we want. There are other tools we will focus on that will assist you in bringing more clarity to what you REALLY want and desire.

Module 3

Listen: How to Fuel Your Presence Activity

S
I
L = LISTEN
E
N
C
E

In our fast-paced world today, how often do we pay attention to our senses as messages from the Universe or the answers to our prayers and intentions? This week I invite you begin to pay closer attention to what you notice through your senses. Could there be signs right in front of you that you don't see because you are not stopping to notice?

Allow yourself time to deepen into your sense as a way to refuel yourself so that you can learn to be more present in each and every moment.

Exploring Your Senses: Pick just one and spend time noticing.

SIGHT

- Observe a sunset
- Walk in nature
- Observe a Facebook quote or picture that catches your eye

SOUND

- Listen to fav song
- Don't turn on the TV and notice what you hear
- Listen to a motivation

SMELL

- Breathe
- Use an essential oil
- Enjoy the aroma of cooking or baking

TASTE

- Take 15 minutes to enjoy and eat your favorite dessert
- Eat a piece of chocolate
- Savor a strawberry

TOUCH
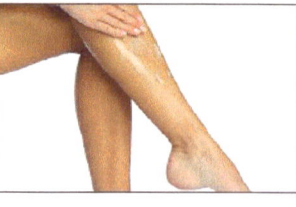
- Rub lotion on your body
- Have a family member rub your neck or feet
- Enjoy taking a bath or shower (don't rush)

After you allow yourself to enjoy and explore your senses, notice if you REALLY allow yourself to enjoy, or are you rushing through so that you can get something else done? Are you multi-tasking and thinking of the next thing, or are you able to relax and be in the present moment.

If you are able to relax in the moment. What do you notice afterwards?

Module 4

S
I
L = EMOTIONS
E
N
C
E

Emotions: Feelings Activity

It is important to create awareness of our feelings. This work sheet is a reference document for how you can look at your feelings and use them as inputs to where you are or are not in alignment with your soul's purpose. Taking responsibility for understanding how to work with our emotions instead of against them will help in how you can communicate more effectively with others, as well as yourself. How are you showing up? Are you coming from a heart centered authentic place or are you coming from a head centered ego place? All judgement comes from a place of fear. When you are judging someone you are in an ego centered place. Acceptance comes from observing and asking for support with no judgement.

Reflection—Think and reflect on the following:
- Do you ever bury your feelings and emotions?
- Do you ever judge what you are feeling? Do you criticize yourself for your feelings?
- Do you have a hard time finding the right words to express what you are feeling?
- Do you not share or express what you are feeling because of what others might think?
- Do you think it is not appropriate to share or express what you feel?
- Do you think it is no one else's business to know what you feel?
- Do you blame yourself for feelings you feel are "wrong" to feel?

There are two different approaches in how we communicate:
1. **Heart centered:** This is from our authentic self. When we are being honest and truthful about our experience and listen to our inner voice.
2. **Head centered:** This is when we communicate from the ego. There is typically some type of blame involved. Whether we are blaming someone else or we are blaming ourselves for what is showing up.

It is important to understand where we are coming from when communicating and sharing emotions, whether we are communicating with ourselves or with others.

Use the Model on the next page when feelings show up for you and determine how you respond or react to what is showing up for you.

Module 4

Emotions: Feelings Activity

S
I
L
E = EMOTIONS
N
C
E

The Heart Centered vs. Head Centered Model (Based off of the NVC Distinctions Model)

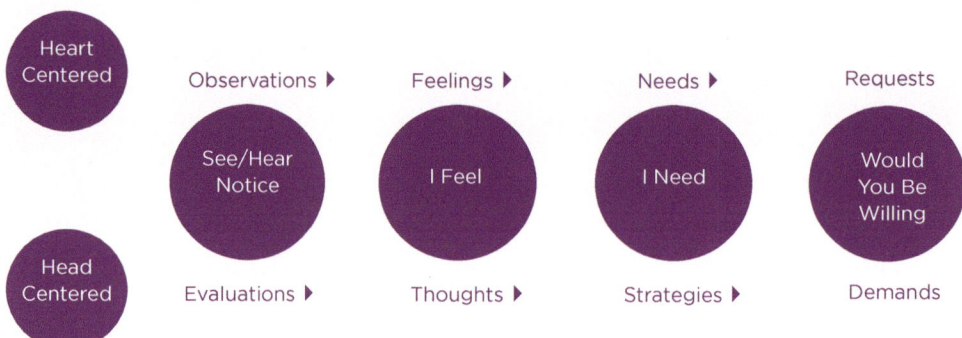

1. Are we observing or evaluating? When we come from a heart centered place, we are merely observing what is showing up for us. There is no judgement just pure awareness. When we come from a head centered place, we are making judgments about our feelings.
2. Are we discussing feelings or thoughts? When communicating, are you sharing TRUE feelings, or are you sharing thoughts and judgements about the feelings? Tap into what it is that you are experiencing.
3. Are we stating needs or strategies? Are you trying to FIX someone by recommending strategies or are you stating and claiming what it is that you REALLY need. Sometimes we deflect and come up with excuses or reasons not to ask for what we really need.
4. Are we asking or demanding? Are you asking for and making a request for what you need, or are you demanding it. There is a big difference in how your energy is felt when you are coming from a heart centered place and asking, vs. when you are showing up in ego and demanding something.

You can use this model both at the office and at home. When you are able to connect in a more heart centered space in the office, you will see a shift in how you show up and how people interact with you. The same goes for how you connect with family members as well. If you come across as demanding, you may feel resistance from others, however, when you show up authentic and create healthy boundaries you gain the credibility and respect that you crave.

Module 4

Emotions: Feelings Activity

S
I
L = EMOTIONS
E
N
C
E

EMOTIONS REFERENCE CHART

Below is an emotions chart to use as reference as you start to identify some of the feelings that might be coming up for you. If our needs are NOT being met, then we tend to have "negative feelings". If our needs are being met, we have "positive" feelings.

FEELINGS WHEN NEEDS ARE NOT BEING MET					FEELINGS WHEN NEEDS ARE BEING MET			
Hostile	Hate	Repulsed	Vindictive	→	Energetic	Elated	Giddy	Silly
Angry	Enraged	Livid	Mad	→	Excited	Alive	Animated	Passionate
Annoy	Bitter	Frustrated	Peeved	→	Inspired	Amazed	Thrilled	Radiant
Upset	Unsettled	Agitated	Disturbed	→	Joyful	Amused	Happy	Pleased
Tense	Nervous	Overwhelmed	Stressed Out	→	Relaxed	At Ease	Carefree	Comfortable
Afraid	Concerned	Frightened	Scared	→	Curious	Adventurous	Intrigued	Fascinated
Vulnerable	Cautious	Guarded	Helpless	→	Confident	Empowered	Proud	Secure
Confused	Lost	Hesitant	Skeptical	→	Engaged	Involved	Absorbed	Alert
Embarrassed	Ashamed	Guilty	Humiliated	→	Hopeful	Expectant	Encouraged	Optimistic
Longing	Envy	Jealous	Yearning	→	Grateful	Appreciative	Thankful	Moved
Tired	Exhausted	Depleted	Worn Out	→	Refreshed	Renew	Rest	Restore
Disconnected	Bored	Detached	Numb	→	Affectionate	Close	Tender	Compassionate
Sad	Depressed	Disappointed	Discouraged	→	Peaceful	Blissful	Mellow	Serene
Shocked	Surprised	Startled	Disbelief	→	Relieved	Complacent	Cool	Trusting
Pain	Anguish	Devasted	Heartbroken	→	Content	Cheerful	Glad	Fulfilled

If you want to change the outcome of any situation it first begins with the mind.

- What is the thought that is triggering the emotional response? And what is the current Result/Outcome?
- How can you shift your thoughts to create a new feeling and an actionable end result that is positive?
- When you are able to see the opposites of various feelings, this can be a guide to help you reframe your thinking and create results that your authentic self TRULY desires.

Module 5

S
I
L
E
N = **NEW BEGINNINGS**
C
E

The Power of Choice Activity

Every change in life happens with a CHOICE. We either choose to act or we choose not to act, but NOT ACTING is a choice in itself. Procrastinating and waiting is a choice. Taking a risk is a choice. What kinds of choices are you making? Are your fears or subconscious beliefs holding you back? What is STOPPING you from making a decision? This is a part in the process where many times individuals get stuck. We get stuck in indecision or procrastination and sit in the vicious hamster wheel. Change can happen in a second when you make the choice to do so.

What comes first, Courage or Confidence? What do you VALUE? What do you really DESIRE? What commitment are you ready to make?

To show you the value of how this works, let's complete an activity where we reflect on some past decisions that we have made. I want you to go through the process and outline for yourself what happened in each step. You will begin to see some patterns emerge. You will see how in the past you have made decisions and built your confidence along the way. You can use this as a model for future decisions. Knowing that when you make a commitment, that you will courageously take the next easiest actionable step, one simple step at a time.

STEP 1 : Commit and decide to act on the challenge or opportunity. When you make a choice, you make a commitment to yourself that you intend to see that decision through.

STEP 2: Have the courage to take action on your commitment. When you commit to a choice, you might still be nervous, in fact, you probably are. That is ok. What thoughts and fears may have showed up for you? What did you do about them?

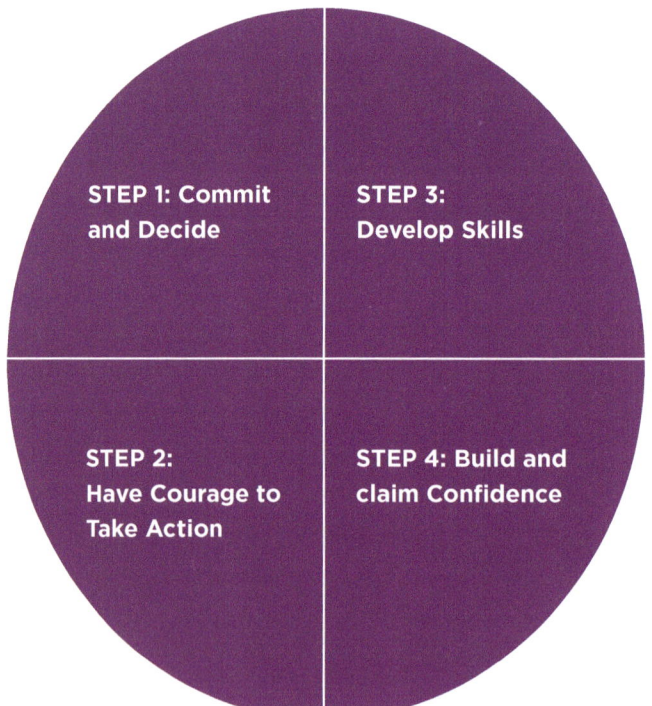

STEP 3: Use your courage to develop the necessary skills and acknowledge your efforts. Reflect on the skills you built during the process and praise yourself for your progress.

STEP 4: Build and claim the confidence that results from learning the skills, exercising action and making the commitment. Reflect on how you feel and declare your confidence in your decision and the skills you built during the process.

What is something that you want, that you have not acted on yet? What decision could you make that would shift something in your business or personal life? Claim what you DECIDE TODAY.

Module 6

How Radical Responsibility Increases your Leadership Influence C- Choice

S
I
L
E
N
C = CHOICE
E

We always have a choice on whether we will hold onto something or if we are ready to let something go. It is much easier to blame others and/or hold onto some kind of resentment or bitterness when things do not go as expected. Take a moment to reflect on an event(s) and/or person where you have a hard time letting go. Is there something or someone you need to forgive in your life? Name 3 people you need to forgive or things you need to let go of in your life.

1. _____
2. _____
3. _____

Forgiveness will allow you the freedom to let something go and create more space for something new. Before you can begin to forgive others, you must take a closer look at yourself. What things do you say to yourself? What things do you say about yourself? Have you thought about the concept of forgiving and letting go of any strongholds you have placed on yourself?

Have you ever said things to yourself like? (Check all that apply)

_____ I am not good enough
_____ Hard work means I have to sacrifice
_____ I am not talented enough
_____ I can't afford to follow my dreams
_____ My family wouldn't approve
_____ It's against my faith

_____ I can't do it alone
_____ I don't have the time
_____ I don't have the money
_____ My spouse wouldn't approve
_____ I don't know how
_____ It's not worth it

Thought Provoking Questions (Check all that apply)

_____ Do you believe in yourself?
_____ Do you regret things you have done?
_____ Do you regret things you haven't done?
_____ Do you have dreams that are buried?
_____ Are you holding on to resentment?

_____ Do you blame your parents?
_____ Do you expect others to change?
_____ Do you blame others?
_____ Are you too hard on yourself?
_____ Do you fear being imperfect?
_____ Do you fear what others think?

Module 6

S
I
L
E
N
C = CHOICE
E

How Radical Responsibility Increases your Leadership Influence C- Choice

Speaking or thinking thoughts like these are like praying and setting intentions for things that you don't want. If you have checked off one or more of these statements, begin some self-reflection to see where you may need to make a choice and let go of something you have been holding onto.

Choosing forgiveness is not just being sorry for a wrong doing. It is the intentional and voluntary process by which a person undergoes a change in feeling & attitude regarding an offense and lets go of negative emotions with an increased ability to wish the person well.

When you begin the self-reflection process and decide to take action, you begin to take Radical Responsibility for your life.

Building, Maintaining and Embodying Confidence

Module 7

S
I
L
E
N
C
E = EXPRESS

So often we forget to take time out to recognize our own accomplishments and celebrate who we are. Sometimes we have a hard time tooting our own horn and appreciating the little accomplishments along the way. We can be our own worst critic.

List 5 things you want to celebrate from this week or this month. It is important to stop and notice not just the big things, but the little things as well.

What am I proud of?	Reason this is so amazing

What can you do to celebrate your accomplishments?

1.

2.

3.

4.

5.

What Others Are Saying...

I truly appreciated how wonderfully accessible the information was in Jen's book. Jen's personal revelations help me see how progress can unfold and gives me hope for myself. SILENCE is so important and now has even more meaning.

~Karen M. Carlson, LMT Be Well Massage,
www.bewellandrenew.com

From the very first page of her book, Jen's words resonated with me. Her gentle approach to tapping into our own wisdom and power is beautifully explained and expanded upon through her use of key concept words which make up the word SILENCE. I find myself looking forward to quiet meditation using the powerful affirmation guide at the end of her book. I am discovering my true self and my own desires through quiet reflection and Jen's guidance.

~Erin Harris, Customized Jewelry,
www.elmharris.com

Working with Jen was a life changing experience: She gave me tools I needed to quiet my mind, listen to my inner voice and be present in the moment. I've learned how to take better care of myself and fulfill my own desires so I can be more effective in my personal and professional life. I learned how to quiet my mind and experience SILENCE.

~Teresa Perdue, Project Manager

Jen's women's circle felt like an emotional cleanse with a spiritual infusion. I'm already looking forward to the next time. She creates a safe sacred space for women to share our hearts with each other and more fully explore our true selves.

~Paula Banno , Marketing Consultant,
www.Resultspjb.com

Before working with Jen, I was a sweats and no makeup kind of gal. Now I feel so good about myself, I look forward to picking out an outfit every day. I didn't realize that my actions and subconscious feelings were suppressing me from my true heart and soul. I was able to let go of so many hang-ups. I was able to find my true self, while being content, fulfilled confident and free all at the same time.

~Cindy Tschosik, Content Writer,
www.soconnected.com

Jen inspired me to take action to loving and accepting myself again. I lost over 45 pounds and reduced my blood pressure and cholesterol. I gained a new level of confidence and began wearing dresses again. Jen creates a comfortable and relaxed atmosphere that brings a sense of openness and trust to all. She guided me through exercises to reconnect with my feminine energy. I feel more alive as a woman.

~Beth Majerszky, Life Coach and Retreat Leader,
www.coach-beth.com

In working with Jen, I experienced a level of happiness, calm and contentment that I didn't know was possible. An all-around warm fuzzy feeling. We experienced laughs, tears and several moments of pure joy. Her programs allowed me to be more courageous in seeking out speaking opportunities which led to landing my dream job. I feel free to live out the truth of who I am without fear, judgment, or being ashamed of my feminine beautiful energy and sexuality.

~Jennifer M. Cross Holistic Health Counselor,
www.AuthenticLivingWellness.com

Programs & Services

Programs and Services

- Single Engagements: Lunch and Learns, Half and Whole Day Workshops
- Awaken Your Presence E-Course Program—7 Keys to Creating More of What You Really Desire
- Emerging Leader Coaching: 3,6, and 12 month Freedom Keys Mastery Programs
- 1:1 Executive Coaching: Personal Intensive Coaching
- Off-site Retreats—Improving Personal Effectiveness through Embodied Leadership

Sought after Speaking

- Awaken Your Presence: 7 Keys to Creating More of What you Really Desire
- The Power of Confidence: The 4 Secrets to Overcoming Fear and Claiming Your Power
- The Power of Influence: How to Build Your Confidence, Set Clear Boundaries and Elevate Your Impact
- Pleasure without Apology: How to Stop People Pleasing and Invite More Pleasure into Your Life

If you are ready to bring a powerhouse speaker into your organization or if you are a woman who is ready to step up your game, schedule a complementary consult today. Contact Jen at (331) 444-2281 or sign up directly at https://secure.scheduleonce.com/jenbugajsky.

About Jen

"Listen to the whispers, learn to embrace silence and live a life of presence and purpose."

Jennifer Bugajsky worked in Corporate America for 20 years and began her journey to becoming a coach seven years ago, when two of her boys had serious health issues and a male senior executive told her she lived in a box and that she needed to wake up and wear her "big girl panties."

Back then, she struggled to DO IT ALL! She was overworked, stressed-out and tired. She gained extra weight and had little-to-no energy. She felt unfulfilled and unsatisfied; her relationships suffered and she didn't like who she saw in the mirror.

Jen has emerged as a fierce advocate for women to discover their voice, declare their confidence and develop an executive presence that attracts the attention they desire, so they can ditch the burnout, increase their performance and have a great influence in their families, organizations and communities.

She believes that strong, authentic female leadership presence is the key to helping organizations thrive in today's competitive business environment and for women to play a bigger game and be confident in asking for what they REALLY want and desire.

Jen is an inspirational speaker, author, singer, songwriter, and women's leadership development coach. She is a Board Certified Health Coach and is trained in the Art of Feminine Presence™. Jen is the co-author of the international best-selling book *Rapid Change*.

Jen believes when you focus on your own fulfillment, you are more present to everything.

Notes

www.ingramcontent.com/pod-product-compliance
Lightning Source LLC
LaVergne TN
LVHW072118070426
835510LV00003B/109